Fishing Fun

by **Francis McCall** and **Paul Richardson**

photographs by **Francis McCall**

Bebop Books

An imprint of *LEE & LOW BOOKS Inc.*

Dad drives us to the river.
We park the car.
Dad says, "This is the best spot
to fish."
We unpack our fishing tackle.
"Now we just need to get some
worms," I say to my brother Arian.

3

"Brandon, why do we need worms?" Arian asks.
"We need worms for bait to catch the fish," I say.
Together we dig up a clump of dirt full of worms.

"Cool!" Arian squeals. "They're wiggly!"
"That's the way the fish like them," I say.
We put the worms in a can with some damp dirt.

Dad ties a hook, a sinker, and a bobber
onto the line on each fishing pole.
"Time to bait your hooks," he says.
"No way!" says Arian. "I'm not going
to put a worm on my hook."
Dad and I laugh.
Dad puts the worms on our hooks while
Arian and I watch.

Now it's time to fish!
We cast our lines into the water.

We hold our poles over the water.
We watch, and wait, and wait.

Finally the tip of my pole jerks.
My pole bends and my bobber goes
under the water.
"I have one," I yell. "I have a fish!"
"Look," Arian says. "Brandon's fish!"
"It's a big one," Dad says.

Suddenly my pole straightens out.
The fish drops off my line.
"Oh no," I say. "My fish is gone!"

I reel in my line.
My fish got away.
Even the worm is gone from my hook.

"That fish was really big," Arian says.
"It was this big."
"No, no," Dad says. "It was twice as big as that."
"Oh no," I say. "It was even bigger than that. It was this big!"

"Brandon, you know what?" Dad says.
"The one that gets away is always the biggest."
"It was huge!" I say.

"Throw your line in the river again," Dad says. "Right," I say. "I bet there's an even bigger fish out there."

Soon all three of us have our lines
in the water again.
Then Arian's pole bends.
"I have one," he yells. "It must be
a big one!"
"Pull back on your pole," I say.
"Reel it in."

Arian reels and reels.
He pulls a shoe out of the river!

"What kind of fish is that?" Arian says.
We all laugh.

I take the shoe off Arian's line.
"I'll put it in the bucket," I say "Mom likes
to know what we catch."

Arian giggles.

"Who cares if we catch any fish," he says.

"Fishing is a lot of fun!"

Things You Need to Go Fishing

worms

fishing pole/rod

bobbers

fishing line

tackle bag

bobber

reel

sinkers

sinker

hook